Mewsings

Mewsings

Exploring the Feline Mystique

Text & Photographs by Fiona Green

Willow Creek Press

Published by Willow Creek Press
P.O. Box 147, Minocqua, Wisconsin 54548

For information about custom editions, special sales, premium and corporate purchases,
please contact Jeremy Petrie at 800-850-9453 or jpetrie@willowcreekpress.com.

Editor/Design: Andrea Donner

Library of Congress Cataloging-in-Publication Data: To come
Green, Fiona, 1964-
  Mewsings : exploring the feline mystique / Fiona Green.
      p. cm.
  ISBN 978-1-59543-809-6 (hardcover : alk. paper)
  1. Cats--Miscellanea. I. Title.
  SF445.5.G74 2008
  636.8--dc22

                              2007046867

Printed in China

With Thanks...

To Mirek, my husband and fellow cat lover,
for always encouraging my creative endeavours.

To Hamish, Angus, Dougal, Climie, Marvin, and Tiger
for teaching me to appreciate the beauty of cats
and inspiring me to write this book.

To Ann and Tom for their valuable insight and editorial input.

Preface

Growing up in Scotland the only pets I owned were a goldfish and a tortoise; it wasn't until my mid twenties that I discovered the wonderful world of cats and officially became a "cat person." At the time I was studying for a diploma in commercial photography at Dawson College in Montreal, Canada. When a friend asked if I would be interested in adopting two stray kittens, I was hesitant as I knew absolutely nothing about cats. With my husband's coaxing, I agreed to take them on a trial basis. Hamish and Angus, two adorable ginger tabbies, immediately stole our hearts. These perfect little furry creatures were beautiful to watch—whether they were stretching, wrestling, kneading, purring or simply sleeping, and I used dozens of rolls of film trying to capture their every move and expression. Needless to say, I can no longer imagine my life without cats.

When Hamish and Angus tired of posing for me I volunteered to shoot the calendar for the Montreal CSPCA. I had the pleasure of providing photographs for eight calendars and was privileged to meet many wonderful people and their pets along the way.

Through reading about and observing cats I soon gained an understanding of their behavior and an appreciation of all things feline. Having amassed a large portfolio of animal portraits over the years I decided it would be interesting to put together a collection of my favorites with some of the facts I had learned. The end result is this book. It is written as a tribute to the cats who inspired me and is intended to be enjoyed by all who share my fascination with our wonderful feline friends.

Cats Throughout History

Throughout history, society's attitude toward cats has undergone many changes.

Perhaps the best time to be a cat was over 2,000 years ago in ancient Egypt. During this period, cats were greatly respected for their practical value as they made excellent hunting companions and skilled rodent control experts. Over the years the bond between the Egyptians and their felines grew stronger, and cats were no longer simply viewed as useful exterminators but as an integral part of the family. Some religious cults believed that they were associated with the gods and worshipped them accordingly, with many families placing cat statues outside their home to ward off evil spirits.

Cats were so highly revered that if a human killed one, either intentionally or unintentionally, he would be sentenced to death.

When a cat died, members of the household would go into deep mourning, often shaving their eyebrows to publicly display their grief. The mummified cat would be taken for burial to the temple of the cat goddess, *Bast* or *Bastet*. When this temple was excavated in 1888, the preserved bodies of tens of thousands of cats and kittens were found.

Changing Attitudes

Perhaps the worst time in history for felines was the Middle Ages when cats in Europe were associated with evil and witchcraft. Sadly, superstition, fear, and ignorance led to the sacrifice of vast numbers and the population quickly dwindled. With fewer cats around, the number of rodents increased, contributing in part to the spread of the bubonic plague, or Black Death, that ravaged Europe and killed thousands.

During the Renaissance cats regained their place as beloved household companions. Their revival in popularity was no doubt largely a result of the literary movement of the period, as cats were often the subject of choice for artists and authors.

To this day our furry friends have remained an important part of the family—respected, pampered, and adored.

Felis Catus

In Latin the term for the domestic cat is *felis silvestris catus*. The word *felis* is actually derived from the adjective felix, meaning happy.

A male cat is called a *tom* and a female cat is called a *queen*. The correct term for a group of kittens is a *kindle,* while a group of grown cats is a *clowder*.

There is a good chance that you are an *ailurophile*, or cat lover, since you are reading this book. Famous cat lovers include Ernest Hemingway, Theodore Roosevelt, and Sir Isaac Newton.

A person who fears or dislikes cats is an *ailurophobe*. Adolf Hitler, King Henry III, and Napoleon Bonaparte were all ailurophobes.

As a cat lover, it's hard to imagine how anybody could dislike cats!

Catnapping

While experts recommend we should aim for eight hours of sleep per night, cats seem to be of the opinion that more is better, snoozing on average a whopping sixteen hours each day.

The cat's sleep pattern has evolved as a result of her predatory nature. She is always on the alert for her next meal and even when she is asleep, her brain is constantly monitoring the environment for signs of danger.

Cats in the wild are busiest at dawn and dusk when their prey is active. The same is true for domestic cats who often seem to come alive at the end of the day and start racing energetically through the house, for no apparent reason. This period, referred to by many as the "evening crazies," usually coincides with the time we are drifting off to sleep.

Grooming Experts

Cats spend nearly 30 percent of their life grooming themselves. With all this licking they lose a lot of fluid—in fact, they lose almost as much liquid as they do through urination.

Cats will immediately start cleaning and grooming themselves after eating to get rid of any food scent that might give them away. This cleaning ritual protects wild cats from unwelcome predators.

Grooming also allows cats to remove any loose hair from their coats. Once swallowed, the hair normally passes easily through the digestive system. However, if too much is ingested it may be coughed up in the form of a hairball. Since cats love to play games, they may choose to do this during the night, ensuring that a lovely surprise awaits us as we make our way barefoot and bleary-eyed to the kitchen in the morning.

We can help our furry friends eliminate stubborn hairballs by applying a lubricant like Vaseline to their front paws. Bewildered by our actions, their first reaction will be to get rid of the slimy goo by licking their paws clean. Who says you can't outsmart a cat!

On the Prowl

C ats are excellent hunters, combining speed and strength with highly developed senses.

Nowadays, very few domestic cats actually hunt for their supper and more often than not they simply stand next to their empty food dish and watch in amazement as it is magically replenished before their eyes. Nonetheless, we can see from observing their play that the hunting instinct is still there. Kittens clearly derive great pleasure from games that involve hiding behind doors, then running out and pouncing on unsuspecting humans, or batting toy mice around and jumping on them so they can relive the moment of capture over and over again.

If kitty ventures outdoors there is a good chance that she may put her indoor training to the test. When she returns home after a particularly hard evening hunting and drops a dead mouse at your feet, it is difficult to resist the temptation to shriek and climb up on the kitchen counter. Instead of being scolded, however, she should in fact be praised for her thoughtfulness. After all, she is not trying to scare you but is simply showing her love by presenting you with a gift.

Food for Thought

C ats are unable to chew as they cannot move their lower jaw sideways or grind their teeth. Food is usually swallowed whole and processed by the digestive juices.

If you have ever wondered why a cat's tongue feels like rough sandpaper, there is a simple explanation. It is covered with tiny hook-like barbs called *papillae,* which allow her to tear feathers or fur from her prey. The barbs also help remove loose hair from her coat when she is grooming herself.

A cat has only 473 taste buds while humans have around 9,000. Her remarkable sense of smell, however, is thought to be about fourteen times stronger than ours. As well as smelling with her nose, kitty also smells with an "extra sense," called the *Jacobson's organ*, which is located in the roof of her mouth and is connected to the nasal passage.

Bearing this in mind we can perhaps understand why she often decides to pay a visit to the litter box immediately after we have cleaned it.

On the Menu

*C*ats are carnivores and cannot survive on a purely vegetarian diet as their body requires *taurine*, an essential amino acid present in meat.

Many people believe that the healthiest diet for their cat consists primarily of fresh, raw meat as this most closely resembles the diet of cats in the wild. Most cat owners, however, prefer to stick with a diet comprised of both dry and moist commercial cat food. Recognizing that cats, like people, have a variety of tastes and nutritional needs, pet food manufacturers offer a wide selection of tasty morsels to suit every cat from active, growing kittens to sedentary, overweight seniors.

While we may occasionally treat ourselves and indulge in sugary candies, pies and cakes, cats should never be given sweets as this can prove toxic for them. If wild cats don't include muffins and chocolate in their diet, neither should your cat!

Water Basics

*L*ike humans, cats need to stay hydrated and should ideally drink two and a half times the amount of food they eat.

Their water should be changed daily and served in either ceramic or stainless steel bowls. Some cats prefer drinking from a faucet, possibly because they lack the depth perception required for drinking from a bowl.

We should remember that despite the stereotype of a cat enjoying a large saucer of milk, adult cats are lactose intolerant. So when kitty insists she wants to share our bowl of chocolate chip ice cream, we should pay no attention. Remember it's for her own good.

The Athletic Cat

Our furry friends are extremely flexible. While many of us struggle to simply touch our toes, a cat's daily yoga routine includes rolling into a tiny ball and stretching into a straight line with very little effort.

Felines are also great climbers and can scale a tree in seconds. However, as we know, what goes up must come down. This is where the fun begins. Since her claws curve under, a descending kitty is unable to get a good grip and faces a dilemma as to how to return to *terra firma*. Methods employed generally include hugging the tree and sliding backwards, taking a leap of faith, or meowing softly until some kind person fetches a ladder.

When cats do take a tumble their quick reflexes and ability to right themselves in mid-air usually allow them to land on their feet and survive with barely a scratch.

Thanks to their extremely powerful hind legs, most cats can jump as much as seven times their height. For humans this would be the equivalent of jumping over four buses stacked one on top of the other!

Watching a cat run is like watching poetry in motion. A natural athlete, she runs swiftly and effortlessly, moving first her front and back legs on one side, then both legs on the other side, reaching speeds of up to 30 mph—fast enough to earn her a speeding ticket in a school zone.

Leaving Their Mark

Cats are territorial by nature. They also enjoy a regular daily routine. When this routine is disturbed by a traumatic event like a move or the arrival of a new pet, they may become defensive and choose to mark their territory and "property" in a variety of unusual ways.

As anyone with a ruined sofa knows, cats often mark by scratching as the clawing action allows them to transfer their odor through the scent glands on their paw pads. The scratch marks act as a visible warning to other cats to keep away from their favorite chair.

They also mark by rubbing, transferring their scent through glands on each side of their forehead, chin, lips and tail. They tend to use their cheeks or chin when rubbing against furniture while they reserve their forehead for marking their favorite people.

A less pleasant but undeniably effective way of territory marking is through spraying, when cats who feel insecure or threatened decide to urinate, usually on a vertical surface, as a warning to other cats to keep away. Some felines may also choose to leave their feces uncovered in the litter box instead of hiding it as they would normally do.

When you think about it, the scratched sofa really isn't such a big deal!

The Perfect Workout

A scratching post is an invaluable addition to any cat owner's home. As well as giving kitty an opportunity for stress relief and an instant manicure, it also allows her to enjoy a good workout. For cats who are less interested in keeping in shape, a well positioned post by a window provides a perfect perch from which they can observe the world go by.

It is often assumed that a cat uses a scratching post to sharpen her claws. This is not quite true. By scratching kitty is actually removing the outer transparent sheath that grows over her claws.

Providing your little furball with a simple scratching post may prevent your beautiful loveseat from being damaged. It will not, however, protect it from your spilled latte.

Kitty Communication

A lthough we may not admit it, most of us talk to our cats. This does not mean that we are crazy. Researchers have found that the more cats are spoken to, the more they will speak back.

By twelve weeks of age kittens have developed a full vocabulary that consists of over 100 different vocal sounds (dogs can make about ten). These sounds can be split into three groups: vowel sounds, murmuring, and calls of high intensity.

Some breeds, like the Siamese, are more vocal than others and can be very demanding when they fancy a snack or some snuggling.

Amongst one another cats rarely meow. It appears that they reserve this method of communication solely for interacting with humans. We should feel honored that they have developed a whole new language simply to talk to us. If only we were smart enough to understand!

Body Language

While we may find it difficult to interpret our cat's vocal responses we can learn a great deal about her mood and intentions by closely observing her body language.

For example, when cats playing together rub heads, it usually means that they have no intention of fighting. Similarly, if kitty pushes her face against your head, it shows acceptance and affection.

When a cat snores, or rolls over on her back to expose her belly, she is showing that she trusts you and feels quite comfortable.

While most women find their cat's gentle rhythmic snoring to be soothing and would not dare to disturb her slumber, they have no hesitation whatsoever in waking their snoring husbands.

Purrfection

It is estimated that the average cat spends approximately 10,950 hours purring in a lifetime.

While experts do not agree on exactly how cats purr, a popular theory suggests that it is the result of rhythmic impulses to the larynx.

Kittens begin purring when they are nursing and use it as a way of communicating their feelings to their mother. Purring releases endorphins in the cat's brain and usually indicates happiness. However, a cat may also purr when she is distressed or unwell. In such cases purring may be a type of healing mechanism as its frequency lies between 25 and 150 hertz, which researchers have found to be the sound frequency that promotes healing and recovery.

Incidentally, at 26 cycles per second, the cat's purr is comparable to the frequency of an idling diesel engine, but it is so much more relaxing!

Feline ESP

*M*any people believe that cats possess a sixth sense, or a special extra sensory perception that makes them aware of impending natural disasters.

As with other animals, their heightened sensitivity to vibrations, seismic shocks, and sound waves may in part be attributed to their acute hearing, as many natural phenomena generate low frequency sounds below the range of human hearing.

A recent example of this advanced warning system in action was the Tsunami in Thailand and Indonesia in December 2004. While the human toll was high, very few animals perished.

Some cat owners believe that their cat's ESP extends to predicting sports scores and will place bets according to signs their cat has supposedly given them. If there were any truth to this notion, Las Vegas casinos would be teeming with cats!

Catnip

The scientific name for catnip is *nepeta cataria*. A perennial herb and member of the mint family, it is also known as catmint, catswort, catnep, and fieldbalm.

Not all cats are susceptible to the affects of catnip and the reaction of those who are affected varies greatly. On average the "catnip high" lasts around six minutes, during which time cats may roll over it, paw at it, chew it, lick it, jump around, and purr.

Humans can also benefit from catnip although the affect it has on us is quite different. Drunk as a tea it is known to relieve headaches, tummy upsets, and insomnia.

Cat's Eyes

In relation to her body size, a cat has the largest eyes of any mammal. These engaging eyes may be why we find her so bewitching and are ready to indulge her every whim!

Compared to humans, cats lack the ability to see detail in objects viewed up close and, although their field of vision is approximately 185 degrees, they cannot see objects directly under their nose. They are also unable to distinguish a full spectrum of colors and suffer a type of red-green color-blindness, known as *deuteranopia*.

A cat's remarkable night vision, however, is eight times more acute than ours. As a nocturnal hunter, this is far more important to her than being able to select coordinating bedroom accessories!

To protect kitty's eyes, nature endowed her with a third eyelid, known as a *haw* or *nictitating membrane*, which helps prevent dryness and damage.

If you are ever unsure of your cat's mood, look deep into her eyes. If she is frightened or excited they will be large. If she is angry, they will be narrow. If they are square, you should perhaps restrict her time surfing the net.

Exceptional Hearing

C ats have some of the sharpest hearing in the animal kingdom.

While humans can hear frequencies from around 20 hertz to 20 kilohertz and dogs from about 20 hertz to 45 kilohertz, cats can hear frequencies that range from 20 hertz to 65 kilohertz. Mice, incidentally, can hear frequencies up to 95 kilohertz.

Cats are thought to be able to distinguish certain sounds—like a doorbell or the opening of a can of their favorite snack. It is claimed that some clever kitties can even recognize their owner's footsteps from hundreds of feet away.

If this is true, it should give them just enough time to tell the dog to get your slippers ready!

Listen Up

We can tell a lot about a cat's mood by the position of her ears. When she is hunting or stalking prey, they will be pointed forward, listening for new sounds. When she is frightened, they will be laid back flat against her head for protection.

Cats have 32 muscles that control the outer ear. This allows them to rotate their ears independently 180 degrees, and turn them in the direction of sound ten times faster than a dog.

Humans have only six muscles controlling the outer ear and although we are unable to rotate our ears, some talented individuals are able to wiggle them. While this is undeniably highly entertaining, it serves no practical purpose for humans.

The Cat's Whiskers

The scientific name for a cat's whiskers is *vibrissae*. Cats have a total of 24 of these tactile facial hairs, four rows on each side, and they are able to move the upper two rows independently of the lower two.

As well as giving kitty character, her whiskers also serve a practical purpose: their sensitivity to air currents helps her feel her way around in the dark. Being roughly as wide as her body, the whiskers act as a built-in tape measure, allowing her to judge whether or not she can fit through an opening. Needless to say, a cat's whiskers should never be trimmed!

The position of the whiskers is also an indicator of mood. When a cat is happy her whiskers will be relaxed and pushed forward. When her whiskers are pulled back, however, this may mean that she feels angry or threatened.

The expression "the cat's whiskers" originated in the 1920s. During this period, various colorful expressions were coined to describe something of the highest quality. Many of these phrases had a connection to an animal or an animal's body part; for instance "the bee's knees." Nowadays these charming phrases have largely fallen from use and have been replaced by words like "awesome."

A Tall Tail

The domestic cat is the only species able to hold its tail vertically while walking. Wild cats hold their tail horizontally or tucked between their legs.

The position of a cat's tail is often indicative of her mood. When her tail is arched up high it may signify an impending cat fight. When it hangs low it may mean that she is afraid. When faced with a predator or a rival, her tail will often puff up to twice its usual size, creating the illusion that she is bigger than she actually is.

The tail serves a practical purpose as it helps kitty balance her body, particularly when she is falling.

Despite the fact that Manx cats have either no tail or a stumpy tail, they fortunately do not appear to experience any problems with balance.

Hairballs

Most cats have three different types of hair in their coat—an outer layer of guard hairs, a middle layer of awn hair, and an undercoat of down hair.

Certain breeds, like the distinctive Cornish Rex, only have down hair.

Cats generally do a wonderful job of grooming themselves as their saliva contains a type of detergent that cleans their fur. Nevertheless, at times they appreciate a little help in the form of a good brushing or combing. Long-haired cats in particular can benefit from being combed as their beautiful, silky fur easily becomes tangled and matted. While a trip to the groomer will take care of any serious problems, regular brushing sessions at home not only provide a wonderful bonding opportunity, but help reduce the number of coughed up hairballs.

Paws for Thought

Cats do not sweat as we do. When a cat is hot, the only way she can dispel heat is by panting and by perspiring through her nose and the pads on her paws.

While most cats have five toes on their front paws and four toes on their hind paws, polydactyl cats may have as many as seven digits on their front and/or hind paws. Mitten cats, or thumb cats as they are also called, were popular among sailors who believed that the cats' giant paws made them more efficient at catching rodents.

Unlike humans who are more often right-handed than left-handed, more cats appear to be left-pawed than right-pawed.

In Japan, many business owners openly display a statue of a cat, known as the *Menaki Neko*, who appears to beckon with one of her paws. If the cat is holding up her right paw she will supposedly bring luck and prosperity. If she is holding up her left paw, she will hopefully attract customers.

Paws for thought indeed…

Tuna Toothpaste

*L*ike babies, kittens are born toothless. After six weeks they have 26 deciduous teeth. These are replaced between weeks eleven and thirty by 30 permanent teeth, sixteen upper and fourteen lower.

By the time they are three years old, 70 percent of cats develop oral disease. Neglected teeth may show a build-up of plaque which, if left untreated, can cause oral problems and may lead to more serious health issues like organ damage.

Although cats spend a large amount of time grooming themselves, many are reluctant to let you brush their teeth with a toothbrush. Many owners do help their furry friends avoid dental problems by brushing their teeth regularly. Cat toothpaste comes in a variety of delicious flavors including tuna, chicken, and beef.

How Young is Your Cat?

Taking into account a cat's shorter lifespan, specialists have developed a formula for calculating feline age in human years. This formula may help us understand kitty's moods and behavior.

According to the formula, a six-month-old kitten is comparable to a ten-year-old child, while having a one-year-old cat is like having a fifteen-year- old teenager. At two years of age, a cat is comparable to a 24-year-old person.

After two years, we can simply add four years for each cat year to find kitty's equivalent human age.

At seven years old, a cat is considered middle-aged, while a ten-year-old cat is considered old.

It is difficult to guess a cat's age simply from her appearance. Her beautiful face and silky, soft fur allow her to age gracefully without having to resort to plastic surgery.

Kitten Caboodle

While a human pregnancy lasts nine months, the gestation period for cats is a mere nine weeks.

A cat may have her first heat cycle while she is still a young kitten at the age of four or five months. With regular heat periods every few weeks, a female kitty can produce several litters per year. Being super fecund, she may mate with more than one male when she is in heat. As a result, different kittens from the same litter may have different fathers.

On average, a first litter will contain three or four kittens while subsequent litters may contain four or more.

At birth, a kitten weighs about three ounces—almost the same as half a can of tuna, a nectarine, or two tennis balls.

Kitten Little

A cat's growth and development is remarkably rapid. In just a few weeks she transforms from a tiny helpless furball who can do little but purr and cry to an alert, rambunctious kitten, bursting with curiosity and ready to explore the exciting world around her.

It is believed that kittens start dreaming at just over one week old. By two weeks their eyes have opened and they are able to respond to sounds.

By the time they are four weeks old, their hearing is developed and they start to play with their littermates. After only five weeks they can run, stalk, and hunt prey. They are also able to groom themselves.

This is fairly impressive when we consider that many adult humans lack the basic skills necessary to groom themselves and rely instead on professionals who are paid handsomely to take care of their hair, teeth, nails, and other general maintenance.

Feline Facts

According to statistics compiled by the American Pet Association, in 2005, there were around 77 million owned cats in the U.S. and almost 63 million dogs.

Thirty-four percent of American households own at least one cat, and 50 percent of cat owners have more than one cat.

Fifteen percent of owned cats were adopted from an animal shelter. Eighty-four percent of domestic cats have been spayed or neutered.

According to the pet identification company, Bow Wow Meow, the most popular names for a male cat in 2007 were Max, Sam, Simba, Charlie, and Oliver, while the favorite names for females were Sassy, Misty, Princess, Samantha, and Lucy.

That Kitty in the Window

Americans are great animal lovers and spend almost $41 billion on their pets annually. According to the ASPCA, the various costs involved in owning a cat amount to around $700 for the first year.

Thereafter, annual veterinary care for a healthy cat is about $100 to $200, approximately the same as the cost of a year's supply of cat litter or a year's supply of cat food.

The American Pet Association estimates that in 2005 almost 40 million cats received Christmas gifts from their owners (figures are not available for the number of cats who reciprocated). While many of these gifts were inexpensive toys, some pampered pets received extravagant jewelry, designer outfits, and makeovers.

Of course, as ailurophiles, we never count the cost. After all, a cat's love is priceless.

Record Breakers

The official record for the largest domestic cat goes to a tabby named Himmy in Queensland, Australia, who weighed 46 pounds, 15.25 ounces.

The oldest living cat on record is Baby from Duluth, Minnesota; when this book went to press, Baby was 37 years old.

In 1970, Tarawood Antigone, a four-year-old Burmese in Oxfordshire, England, gave birth to a litter of nineteen kittens, of which fifteen survived.

The prize for the most prolific cat goes to Dusty from Bonham, Texas, who gave birth to 420 kittens over seventeen years. She supposedly stopped when family reunions became too much for her!

Lost and Found

Every year over 60,000 pets are lost or stolen in the United States. It is estimated that one in three pet owners have at some time lost a beloved, furry family member.

To speed up the process of being reunited with your wandering feline, it is recommended that she wears a tag containing pertinent contact information at all times. Microchipping is also helpful in the event that her tag should fall off.

Clearly the easiest way to prevent a cat from disappearing is quite simply to keep her indoors. If she has never known the outdoor life, she won't miss it. Alternatively, a large exterior enclosure offers the best of both worlds, allowing kitty to enjoy a taste of the outdoors without having to worry about dangers posed by predators, disease, or cars. Of course, depending on the weather and television programming, she might be perfectly happy to stay indoors!

Putting on the Pounds

Obesity is the most common nutritional disease in domestic cats, affecting almost 40 percent of the total population.

It goes without saying that cat owners love their cats unconditionally, even when they start to resemble plump, purring pillows. After all, they don't mind if we pack on a few extra pounds, so why should we complain? We need to bear in mind that while an extra three pounds on a human is a relatively insignificant amount, an extra three pounds on a cat is a cause for concern as feline obesity can lead to other health issues like arthritis, heart failure, diabetes, and urinary tract disease.

Like humans, cats will overeat for a variety of reasons. Eating is often a means of relieving boredom, especially for indoor cats left alone all day. To avoid kitty transforming from an alert, svelte feline into a chubby, lazy furball, a regular feeding schedule is recommended where she is fed two to four times per day. Hiding her dry food in a special cat toy is another effective trick as it not only provides an interesting distraction but encourages her to work for her meals.

Since few cats will voluntarily use a treadmill or stairclimber to keep in shape, introducing more play sessions will help burn those extra calories.

Feral Cats

It is estimated that there are around 70 million feral cats in the United States alone. In an attempt to control the feral cat population, many organizations and volunteers have adopted a "TNR" policy where feral cats are trapped, neutered, and returned to their environment. While it is possible to tame a feral cat, this process becomes increasingly difficult after the age of six weeks.

In theory, a pair of mating cats could produce sixteen kittens within a year. Within two years, if nature runs it course, this number could grow to 128. In three years the total could increase to 512. Within six years the number of furry felines could potentially reach a staggering 67,000.

This is a fairly convincing argument to spay or neuter our pets. After all, who has room for 67,000 cats in their home?

Exploring Our World

Feral cat colonies exist throughout the world. Many are found in idyllic settings such as the Greek Islands where cats roam freely around harbors, parks, churches, and monasteries. At meal times they can often be found on restaurant patios waiting patiently to receive tasty food scraps from some kind-hearted soul.

Some cats choose to live in more prestigious locations which undoubtedly gives them bragging rights in their encounters with other strays. In Canada, for example, a feral colony has been a fixture for many years on Ottawa's Parliament Hill. Cats there are fed by a volunteer, treated by local veterinarians, and visited and photographed by thousands of tourists annually.

Rome, Italy, is perhaps the city with the largest feral cat population in the world. Many can be seen relaxing in the grounds of the Colosseum and the Largo Argentina, where a cat sanctuary is home to over 300 felines.

In Florida, almost 60 cats live around the Hemingway House and Museum, nearly half of which are polydactyl.

Pedigree

No two cats are the same. There are small cats and large cats, fluffy cats and hairless cats, cats with long, bushy tails and tailless cats, cats with extra toes, flat faces, folded ears—the list is endless! They come in an infinite variety of beautiful colors including black, white, grey, red, brown, beige and tortoiseshell, each with their own unique personality.

Approximately one-tenth of owned cats are purebred. There are currently over 100 officially recognized breeds that can be split into four groups: long hair and semi long hair; shorthair; breeds based on mutations; and breeds derived from crossing with wild cats.

While the most popular breeds change from year to year, the following are the top ten in the U.S. in 2006, starting with the most popular: Persian, Maine Coon, Exotic, Siamese, Ragdoll, Abyssinian, Birman, American Shorthair, Oriental, and Sphynx.

Breed Trivia

When you see a tortoiseshell cat there is a good chance that it will be a female as it is estimated that only one in every 1,000 is male. Tortoiseshell cats, or torties as they are also known, have a very distinctive coat that is a beautiful patchwork of black and orange. When a tortoiseshell cat has white markings it may also be referred to as a calico cat.

When Siamese kittens are born they are pure white and their distinct markings—or points—appear as they mature. The color of these points is heat related, with cool areas being darker.

The Ragdoll, which also has these color points, is one of the largest breeds of domestic cat. The interesting name comes from the cat's ability to totally relax when she is picked up (like a floppy ragdoll). Fully grown females typically weigh between fifteen and twenty pounds, while males may weigh up to thirty pounds. That's one heavy kitty!

Superstition

Cats are the subject of many superstitions throughout the world. In Italy, for instance, a sneezing cat is a good omen for everyone who hears it. When moving to a new home in the U.S., it is recommended that you always put the cat through the window instead of the door, so that she will not leave. In southeast Asia, one branch of the Buddhist faith believes that when a person who has reached the highest level of spirituality dies, their soul enters into the body of a cat. It remains there until the cat dies, at which time it enters into Paradise.

In Britain, cats are often relied upon to predict the weather. Some superstitions involving the meteorological cat include: If a cat washes behind its ears, it will rain; a cat sleeping with all four paws tucked under means there is cold weather ahead; when the pupil of a cat's eye broadens, there will be rain.

Of course, in Britain where warm, sunny weather is somewhat rare, there is a good chance that these predictions will be accurate.

Black Magic

In the Middle Ages black cats were associated with evil and many believed that they were witches' helpers who embodied darkness, mystery, and the supernatural. Even today black cats are still regarded in some countries as the bearers of bad luck.

In North America it is considered bad luck if a black cat crosses your path. Allowing one to enter your home, however, is supposed to bring good luck.

When a black cat crosses your path in Russia you can avoid bad luck by changing direction or holding a button between your fingers.

In Britain, a black cat is a welcome sight. Having one cross your path is supposed to bring good luck, while finding one sitting on your porch is a sign of future prosperity.

White Cats

A large majority of white cats with blue eyes are deaf, while white cats with brown eyes are generally not hearing impaired. White cats with only one blue eye are often deaf only in the ear closest to the blue eye.

Cats with white fur and skin on their ears are very prone to sunburn, which can lead to skin cancer. As with humans, preventive measures include using sunscreen or simply staying indoors.

According to superstition, if you dream of a white cat or see one on the road you can look forward to good luck. If you happen to find one sitting on your doorstep just before your wedding, you will supposedly enjoy lasting happiness.

Should you see a white feline at night, however, you may soon experience some bad luck.

Expanding the Family

The arrival of a new cat may disturb the harmony of a household.

When bringing a new feline home, remember that cats are territorial. Avoid throwing them all together in the same same room, expecting them to be instant best friends. In the majority of cases much screaming, chasing, and fur flying is likely to ensue. For an introduction to be effective, it needs to be gradual, and the cats need first to become familiar with one another's scent before actual contact is allowed.

Inevitably there will be some form of physical confrontation as the cats attempt to establish their place in the household hierarchy, but this will generally subside after a few weeks.

Size appears to be of no consequence to cats when picking their wrestling opponents. This leads us to conclude that they are either extremely brave or somewhat crazy!

Atchoo!

It is estimated that almost fifteen percent of humans are allergic to either cats or dogs. The problem is caused by allergens in the animal's fur, saliva, and urine. While medication is perhaps the best option to help deal with allergies, it is possible to significantly reduce the allergens by bathing pets on a weekly basis.

Cats may also suffer from allergies. Signs of a reaction include sneezing, scratching, itching, and vomiting.

When a new partner is found to be allergic to the family pet, this poses a huge dilemma: whether to get rid of the pet or the partner. Needless to say, the partner does not always win.

Cats vs. Humans

While humans can be clearly identified by their fingerprints, in the feline world, cats can be identified by their unique noseprint.

A cat's brain accounts for approximately 0.9 percent of her total body weight, (depending, of course, on the weight of the cat), while a human brain accounts for around two percent of total body weight.

Both humans and cats have identical regions in the brain responsible for emotion.

Humans and cats can hear a similar range of low sounds, but cats have a much greater ability to hear very high notes.

Cats have 230 bones in their body while humans have 206.

A cat's heart beats about twice as fast as a human heart—on average, 120 times per minute when she is resting and 240 when she is active.

Cat Therapy

Cats improve our quality of life. As well as being wonderful, low maintenance companion animals who constantly entertain us with their antics, they are actually good for our health. Research has proven that the simple act of stroking a cat not only feels good but can improve our physical and mental well-being by lowering our heart rate and blood pressure.

Aware of the positive effects of animals on our psyche, many institutions like nursing homes and hospitals allow sociable cats to visit patients who are no longer able to have their own pet. The patients benefit from interacting with the friendly felines, while the cats enjoy basking in the attention that is showered upon them.

The relationship between humans and cats is clearly mutually beneficial. We provide them with a home, food, water, and unconditional love. In return all they need to do is purr softly, rub against our leg, and occasionally allow us to share the bed with them.